INSTANT MASSAGE

FOR STRESS RELIEF

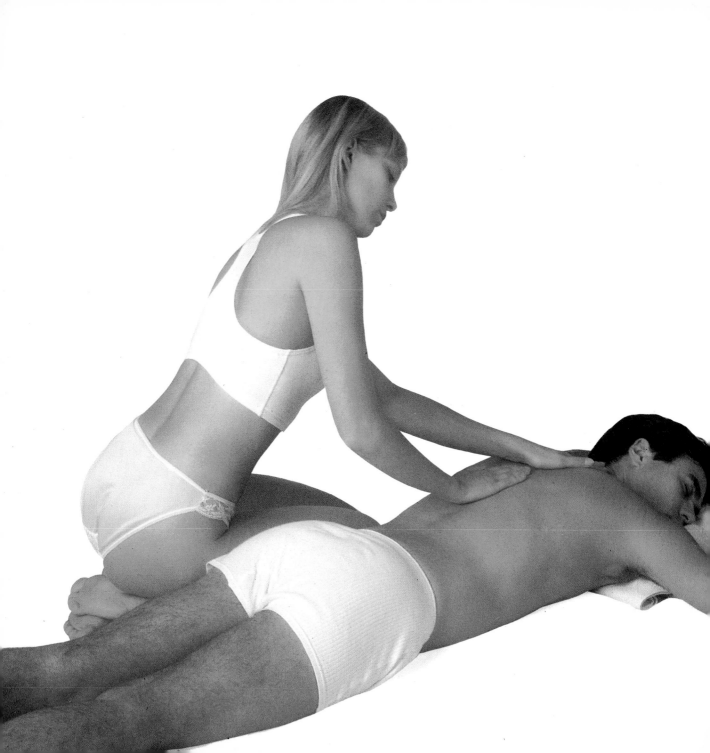

INSTANT MASSAGE

FOR STRESS RELIEF

Easy relaxation

techniques with

step-by-step

massage

MARK EVANS

SPECIAL PHOTOGRAPHY
DON LAST

BARNES
& NOBLE
BOOKS
NEW YORK

This edition published by Barnes & Noble , Inc,
by arrangement with Anness Publishing Limited

2002 Barnes &Noble Books

© 1996 Anness Publishing Limited
Hermes House, 88-89 Blackfriars Road
London SE1 8HA

ISBN 0-7607-3225-6

A CIP catalogue record is available from the British Library

Publisher: Joanna Lorenz
Editor: Fiona Eaton
Designer: Bobbie Colgate Stone
Photographer: Don Last

Printed and bound in China

1 3 5 7 9 10 8 6 4 2

Publisher's note:
The reader should not regard the recommendations, ideas and techniques expressed and described in this book as substitutes
for the advice of a qualified medical practitioner or other qualified professional. Any use to which the recommendations,
ideas and techniques are put is at the reader's sole discretion and risk.

CONTENTS

INTRODUCTION

WHEN YOU COME HOME at the end of the day do your neck and shoulders feel as if they are set in concrete? Does stress leave your back stiff and aching? If you get angry and tense, do you clench your fists, leaving your hands and arms heavy and tired? Anyone who has experienced the physical tensions that can accompany stressful situations will probably not be surprised to learn that massage is one of the most successful ways to relax those painful, knotted muscles.

Most of us almost unconsciously rub tense, aching spots to get some instant relief; correctly performed, massage can have a wonderful effect, not just on the muscles themselves but on our whole sense of well-being. Touch is one of the most crucial, and yet often neglected, senses, and the need for human touch remains constant throughout life.

In the last thirty years, many studies have looked at the importance of touch in human development. Dr Saul Schanberg of Duke University in North Carolina and Dr Tiffany Field from the University of Miami have carried out research on premature babies. The babies who were gently stroked for 45 minutes a day were nearly 50 percent heavier after ten days than non-stroked babies, and were also more active, alert and responsive.

Systematic, caring touch through massage movements has been shown to encourage the

A massage using pure vegetable oils can soothe and comfort the whole person.

release of endorphins – chemicals that affect development in children and emotional and physical well-being in adults. This can work for giver and receiver alike: older, single people are often advised to have a pet to stroke regularly, in order to keep themselves healthier. Studies show that people who experience frequent touch live longer and have fewer ailments.

Professional massage can be an effective treatment for a range of physical problems and is a wonderfully relaxing experience. Many simple techniques can also be used at home to help ease both your own and other people's tensions. By following the suggestions in this book, you can reassure, relax and comfort your family or friends in a way that no non-touch therapy can do. When you consider that an area of skin the size of a coin contains over three million cells, 50 nerve endings and some 3 feet of blood vessels, you can see how much therapeutic impact touch can have on people.

One of the great advantages of massage is that it can be adapted to virtually any situation. You can do it with a partner, and it is almost as effective if you do it on yourself. Some of the actions are versatile enough to apply not only at home

Therapeutic touch can do more than a thousand words to aid healing.

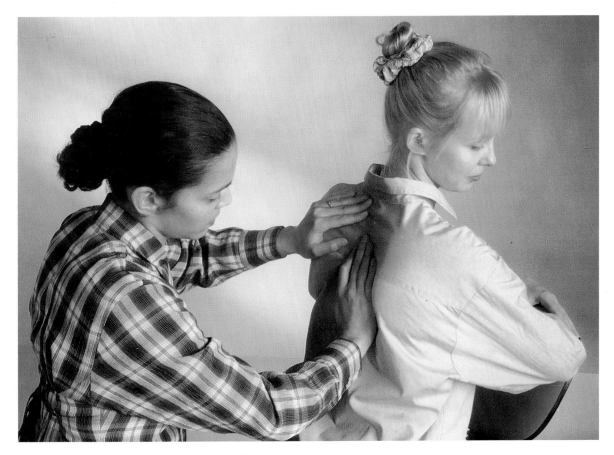

but also in the workplace or even on a bus, since it is not essential for you to be naked or even partially clothed for your tired, aching muscles to be massaged. Massage through clothes is also effective, although a little more pressure may need to be applied. The massage sequences in this book are designed to be versatile. You can

Massage can be adapted to almost any situation with instant benefits.

either apply a particular sequence to help to ease specific muscular aches or, if you have more time, combine several sequences for a relaxing all-over body massage.

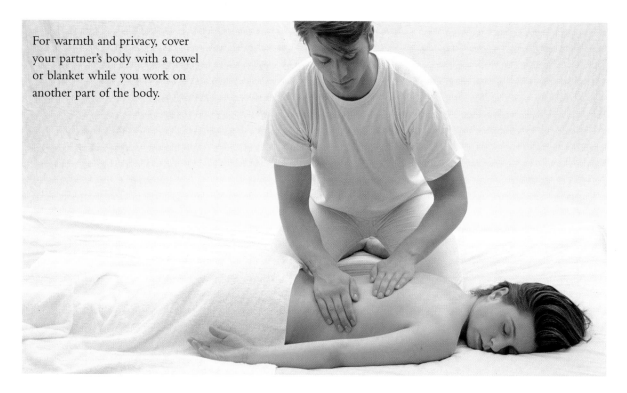

For warmth and privacy, cover your partner's body with a towel or blanket while you work on another part of the body.

Placing your hands on someone else can be one of the most direct ways to make contact with their inner being, and shared touch with your partner helps to make your relationship grow and deepen. Many people nowadays find that their lives are too rushed and stressful to keep the spark going in their relationships; creating a little space each week for an unhurried massage session can rekindle that flame and restore the closeness that we want and need with our partner.

Giving a massage to another person is a privilege, as you are being allowed to make direct contact with him or her. Just placing your hands on someone else's body can give them a strong sense of relaxation and can release blocked energy. It is also an opportunity to connect with the energy of another person and can increase your own sensitivity. All in all, one of the best routes for deeper relaxation, more vitality and greater self-awareness is through massage.

CAUTION:

The massage movements suggested in this book are well-established, safe techniques for working on the body, but there are a few occasions when massage is not appropriate. If your massage partner has a health problem and you are unsure whether or not to do any massage, always seek medical advice. Be particularly careful before giving massage to someone who is pregnant, elderly or frail, or to children. **Remember, if in doubt, don't!** As a rule, **avoid massage** on a person who has:

• An acute infection, or is running a fever
• An area of acute inflammation
• A skin condition such as severe acne or boils
• Large areas of bruising
• Circulatory problems such as varicose veins
• High blood pressure
• Scar tissue from recent surgery

Massage, whether on yourself or on your family and friends, should be a pleasant experience. Sometimes aching muscles can feel tender when massaged, although people usually describe this as a "good" ache and are happy to be worked on; if anyone complains of pain or discomfort, ease up or stop the massage. The treatment should always be an enjoyable one.

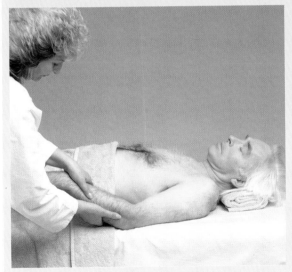

Older people need massage too. Be gentle, and make sure they are comfortable.

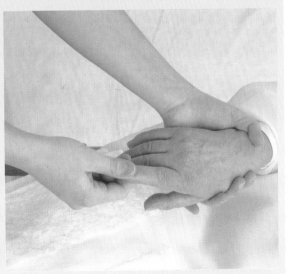

If the person is frail, apply light pressure, and start with areas like the hands.

Preparing for Massage

Creating the right environment and space for treatment can contribute to making massage an even more relaxing and beneficial experience. Before you start, make sure that the room is pleasantly warm and the area for massage is padded enough for your partner to be truly comfortable. Have some towels or a sheet handy to cover areas not being worked on – remember that if you are working on the floor, drafts can give exposed flesh very unrelaxing goose-pimples. If

you are using oil, place it in a convenient spot where you can reach it easily without the risk of knocking it over.

Preparing yourself is important too; physically, this means removing watches and jewelry from your hands and wrists and wearing loose, comfortable clothing, ideally short-sleeved. Try to do a few stretches and take a few deep breaths to help you to feel calm; if you give a massage when you are tense yourself, this may be transmitted to your massage partner. This can work the other way around too, so feel prepared mentally to let go of any tensions that you feel coming from the other person's body and avoid absorbing his or her stresses.

When using oil, pour it onto your own hands first to warm it up, never directly onto your partner. The oil may be placed in a bowl, glass bottle or squeeze bottle for ease of use. Spread oil slowly onto the body – and then begin.

MASSAGE OILS

Throughout the world, people giving massages have used locally available oils, usually vegetable oils, to help the hands flow and glide over the skin. Olive oil, goose grease, goat butter and other ingredients have been used at times; in parts of Africa a handful of oily dough is used to absorb dirt and toxins off the skin as the massage soothes the muscles.

Some oils are more pleasant and versatile than others, and have a beneficial effect on the skin. Probably the most useful oil, and the one most widely used in professional massage, is that of sweet almond. It is light, non-greasy and easily absorbed by the skin. Grapeseed oil seems to suit oily skins quite well; it is reasonably priced and widely available.

Much thicker, but still useful, is soya oil. For dry skins a little wheatgerm oil (but **not** if the person has a wheat allergy) or avocado oil may be added. Nut oils such as walnut are also rich, but a bit sticky, and do not smell too good on the skin. Sunflower oil may be used for massage if nothing else is available, though it may give a slight hint of salad dressing! Olive oil certainly does, although this was used traditionally in Mediterranean countries. Do **not** use mineral oils – they sit on the surface of the skin and feel very greasy.

Essential oils may be added to these base oils, both for fragrance and their therapeutic effects. These are highly concentrated and should be treated with care; if in doubt do not use them, and if any skin irritation occurs, wash the oil off immediately.

Most essential oils are sold in dropper bottles, and it is imperative that they are used only in a diluted form on the skin. A generally safe level is 1 percent, which is the equivalent of using just one drop of essential oil

to 1 teaspoon of base oil. Do not be tempted to use more than the recommended amount.

For a generally relaxing massage blend, try essential oils of lavender and marjoram in equal amounts in a base vegetable oil. Both of these help to release tense, tired muscles and to induce a warm, relaxed glow.

Lavender oil is one of the most versatile and popular.

CAUTION:
Bergamot oil can increase sensitivity to sunlight.
Do not use before going into bright light.

For a more invigorating, uplifting blend, try essential oils of bergamot and geranium in your massage oil. These have a refreshing effect on the whole system.

To release tensions, and also to help to increase libido, try a dilution of an exotic, luxurious blend of essential oils of rose and sandalwood. This is also wonderful for the skin.

From left to right: sandalwood, geranium, rose and marjoram.

MIXING ESSENTIAL OILS FOR MASSAGE

1 Before you begin, wash and dry your hands and make sure that all your utensils are clean and dry. Have your essential oils ready, but leave the lids on the bottles until they are required. Measure out approximately 2 teaspoons of your chosen vegetable oil.

2 Gently pour the vegetable oil into your blending bowl.

3 Add the essential oil, one drop at a time. Mix gently with a clean, dry cocktail stick or toothpick, to blend.

BASIC STROKES

There are many different kinds of massage movements that have specific effects on the body; the basic strokes that form the main substance of massage can, however, be included in a few categories or types. The pattern of a massage often follows certain fundamental principles. To begin with there is the initial contact; the calm, unhurried and relaxed way that you first touch your massage partner can in itself lay the foundation for a soothing, unwinding experience.

GLIDING

A massage usually starts with slow, broad and relatively superficial movements, leading to deeper and perhaps more specific techniques on smaller areas of spasm or tension. If the person needs invigorating or toning up, then faster movements may be used, and finally more soothing, stretching or stroking movements can help to finish the massage in a relaxed way.

The first and last of the massage movements are often therefore gliding strokes. In professional massage parlance these are called effleurage, and involve long, soothing moves that cover a wide area – for instance, the whole of the back. It is perfectly possible to give a complete massage with these stroking techniques, and for gentle relaxation this may be best.

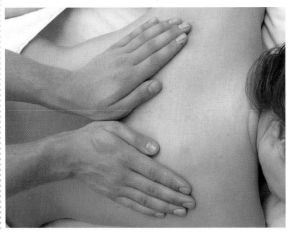

Gliding strokes involve the use of the whole hand in smooth movements.

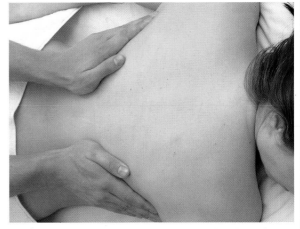

Apply even pressure as you move over the skin. Use plenty of oil.

CIRCLING

An allied form of movement is circling, where the hands move large areas of muscle in a circular motion. Since tension within muscles can produce knotted areas that may need working along or across the length of the fibers, this circular action starts to release the knots before deeper movements are used.

Circling may be carried out with just one hand, or both hands can be used, one on top of the other, for greater depth and stability of action. Like the gliding motions, circling is essentially a slow, relaxing type of movement and should not be rushed.

As with all massage strokes, try to keep your own body comfortable and unstrained, and avoid tensing your hands or arms. Keep a good balance, with your legs slightly apart to enable you to move rhythmically.

A variation on simple circling uses both hands.

Take one hand around in a circle, then the other.

Overlap the hands so that they follow one another smoothly.

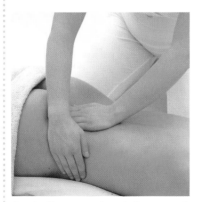

Gradually move the circles up and down the back.

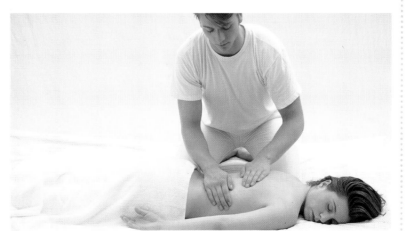

KNEADING

After the recipient has been relaxed by steady stroking or gliding movements, and tense muscles start to release, a professional massage therapist may well begin to use deeper techniques to soften the knotted areas. The general term for many of these movements is petrissage, and they involve a squeezing action to encourage waste matter to be pumped out of the muscles and allow fresh, oxygenated blood to flow in.

The most well-known and widely used of these techniques is kneading. This has some similarities to kneading dough, with the thumbs working on small areas to squeeze the flesh and ease out the tense knots. The movement can be a little tricky to apply correctly at first, but when mastered it is a really useful way to revitalize tired, stiff muscles quickly.

Kneading with alternate hands helps to loosen tense, knotted muscles.

On smaller areas like the calves, use less pressure to avoid discomfort.

20

WRINGING

Another important petrissage-type of movement is wringing, where the action of one hand against the other creates a powerful squeezing action. When performed on the back for example, the person's own spine acts as a block against which the muscles are wrung. This enables the speedy removal of waste matter from tense muscles.

All muscular activity produces potentially toxic waste materials, notably lactic acid. If the person also gets tense and stiff, these wastes are trapped within the muscles, making them even stiffer and more painful. Wringing is a very effective way of encouraging the drainage of lactic acid and other waste matter, which in turn allows new blood to flood in, bringing oxygen and fresh nutrients to each cell.

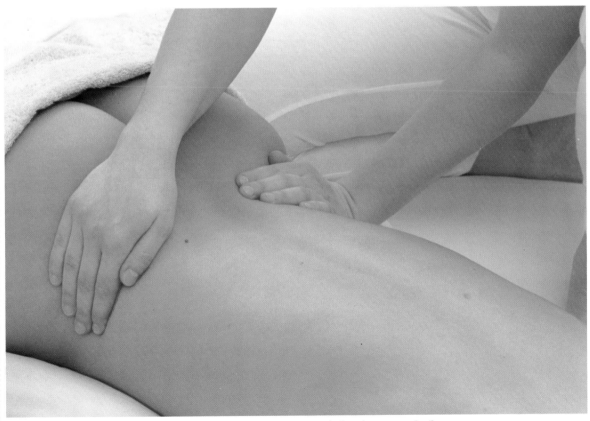

Pushing one hand against the other in a wringing movement helps the removal of waste matter.

PRESSURE TECHNIQUES

As a massage treatment progresses, general techniques such as gliding and circling often change into more detailed and specific work on smaller areas of real spasm. Professional massage therapists may move from petrissage movements to even deeper work with firm pressure using the thumbs or fingers.

In general, pressure techniques are less painful when performed along the direction of the muscle fibers, rather than across them. Pressure is achieved by steadily leaning into the movement with the whole body, not by tensing your hands. The depth of the pressure applied should be adjusted for individual comfort; usually thinner people need lighter pressure.

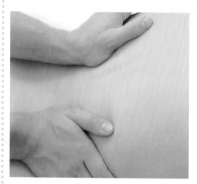

Deeper pressures may be used in professional massage.

The heel of the hand gives a broad, firm effect.

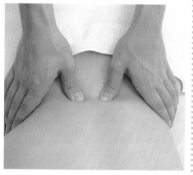

The thumbs can be used to exert the most precise pressure.

The hands often respond well to firm work.

Careful pressure to the neck muscles can give much relief.

CAUTION:
Do not attempt deep work if at all unsure of the effect, or if pain occurs. Underdo rather than overdo massage – effleurage and petrissage movements can make a complete and thoroughly relaxing massage.

PERCUSSION

If someone has a generally sluggish system, or needs invigorating, say before exercise, then faster techniques may be useful. The overall term for these strokes is percussion, or tapotement. Unlike any of the other strokes described here, they need to be performed quickly, to stimulate circulation under the skin and tone the associated muscles.

One of the best known of these movements is hacking, where the sides of the fingers are used to flick rhythmically up and down to create a slightly stinging sensation. Despite being shown frequently in filmed scenes of massage, this and other percussive movements are not at all a major part of massage, but they do have a number of useful effects.

Cupping is another similar stroke which helps to bring blood to the area being worked on. This technique is often used in treating medical conditions such as cystic fibrosis, where a lot of thick, sticky mucus can build up in the lungs. Cupping on the back can help to loosen this mucus enabling it to be brought up and out of the body by the cough reflex.

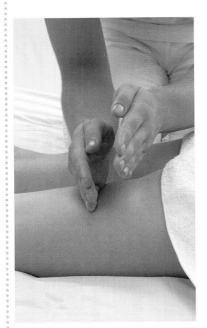

Light hacking movements stimulate the circulation.

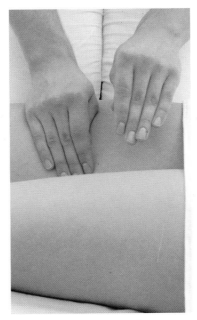

Cupping is another good percussion technique.

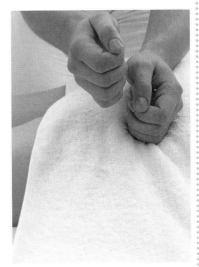

On large muscles, pummeling with loose fists will help to tone and invigorate.

SELF-MASSAGE

One of the nicest things about massage is that you do not need to invest in expensive equipment to do many of the movements, and indeed several strokes can also be used successfully for self-massage. The advantage of working on your own muscles is that you will know exactly how deeply you can press, getting instant feedback from your body about the effects of the massage. Obviously it is not possible to do a complete self-massage, and therapeutically it cannot equal the experience of relaxing on a couch and surrendering yourself to a professional massage treatment. However, you will find that there are many times when you can help yourself

if your body calls out for some physical work to relieve aching, tired muscles.

Many activities inevitably lead to tensions in one part of the body or another, and regular quick massages can help both to ease these tensions and to prevent more chronic aches and pains, or even injury. At any time of the day a short self-massage can help you to feel revitalized and full of energy, and it will reduce the impact of stresses, both physical and mental. So, the next time you are feeling stiff, aching or just completely jaded, follow these simple techniques and put your hands to work to de-stress your whole system — and look and feel younger at the same time!

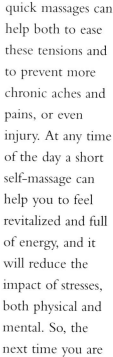

HAND TONIC

Your hands are among the most overworked parts of your body. For some people, such as keyboard operators, machinists and musicians, their hands are not only essential for their livelihoods but they may easily become strained through extended use. Repetitive strain injury may not yet have been fully recognized by the courts in all countries, but it is well-known both by the medical profession and by the workers who suffer its symptoms. Apart from regular breaks in repeated movement actions, self-massage of the hands and fingers can be of tremendous value. Swap hands with each massage technique.

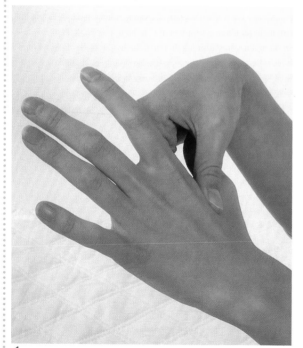

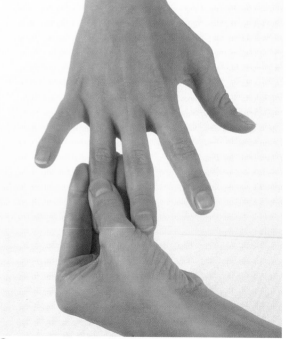

1 To release stored tensions and improve circulation, start by squeezing between each finger in turn with the thumb and index finger of the other hand.

2 Make a rolling movement on each finger, working from the knuckle to the fingertip with firm pressure from the fingers and thumb of the other hand.

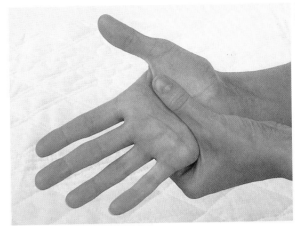

4 Finally, make a firm circling motion with one thumb on the palm of the other hand. This both squeezes and stretches taut, contracted muscles, and should be a fairly deep action; if done too lightly, it is merely ticklish.

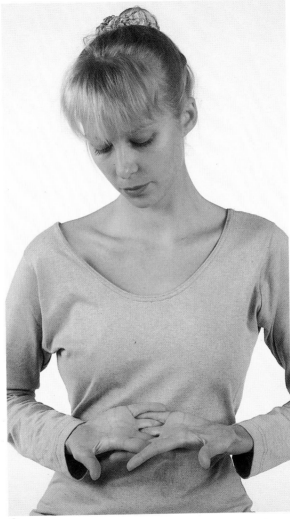

3 Stretch each finger, with a gentle pull to stretch out the tendons that tend to tighten with tension. It is not the intention to "crack" the fingers. Then interlock your fingers and stretch your palms.

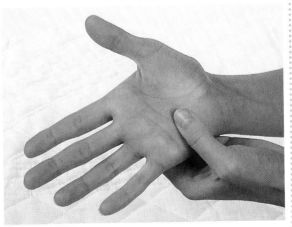

5 Work steadily all over the palm, maintaining a firm pressure the whole time.

27

TENSE NECK EASER

Aching, tense muscles are undoubtedly most frequently experienced in the neck and shoulders. As you get tired, your posture tends to droop and the rounded shape makes your shoulders ache even more. Although it is most relaxing to lie down and have someone else massage them, self-massage of the shoulders and neck can be done anywhere, and without the need to get undressed. Release mounting tension in these areas before your shoulders become permanently hunched up around your ears.

1 A simple movement is to shrug your shoulders, exaggerating their contraction by lifting them up as far as possible and then letting them drop down and relax completely. This is a form of massage that does not even involve using your hands.

2 One of the best massage techniques for removing waste matter from tired muscles and getting fresh, oxygenated blood into them, is kneading. You can do this to yourself – if the arm you are using starts to ache, rest a moment before continuing. Firmly grip your opposite shoulder with your hand and use a squeezing motion to loosen the tension.

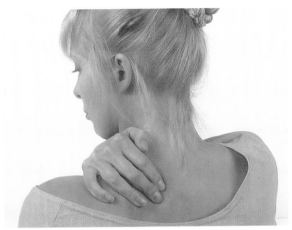

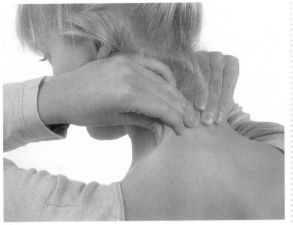

3 Move slowly along the shoulder, squeezing firmly several times. Repeat on the other side, using the opposite hand.

4 With the fingers of both hands, grip the back of the neck and squeeze in a circular motion to help to relax the muscles leading up either side of the neck.

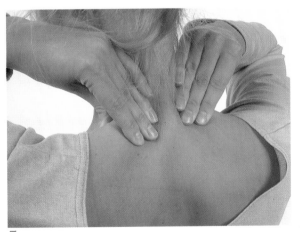

5 Work up as far as the base of the skull, and down again to the shoulders.

6 To work more deeply into the neck, move the thumbs in a circular movement across the neck and right up into the base of the skull. You will feel the bone as you apply moderate pressure.

TONIC FOR ACHING LEGS

Many people such as sales assistants (and indeed shoppers), teachers and hotel doormen spend far too long each day standing still, or barely moving. Numerous occupations ensure a lack of circulation in our legs, which can lead to tired, aching limbs, swollen ankles or cramps. It is, of course, essential for people whose jobs involve a lot of standing to try and move their legs at other times, but a quick self-massage at the end of the day can help considerably in reducing stiffness and sluggishness of blood flow in the legs.

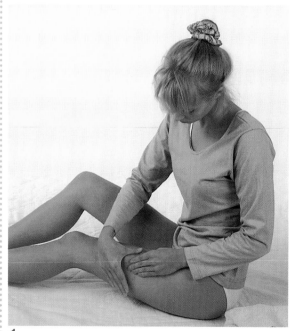

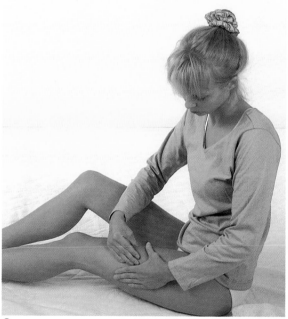

1 Start a leg massage by working on the thighs, so that any fluid retention in the calves will have somewhere to go as the upper leg relaxes. Using both hands, knead one thigh at a time by squeezing between the fingers and thumb.

2 Squeeze with each hand alternately for the best effect, working from the knee to the hip and back. Repeat on the other thigh.

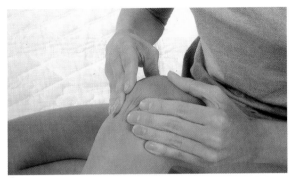

3 Around the knees, do a similar kneading action, but just using the fingers for a lighter effect and working in smaller circles.

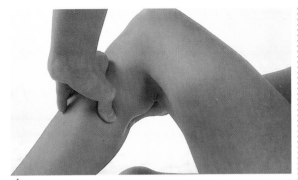

4 Bend your leg, and if possible raise the foot onto a chair or nearby ledge. With your thumbs, work on the back of each calf with a circular, kneading action.

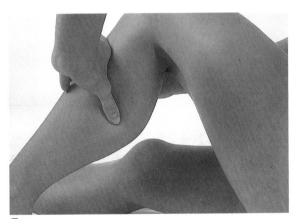

5 Repeat a few times, each time working from the ankle up the leg to the knee.

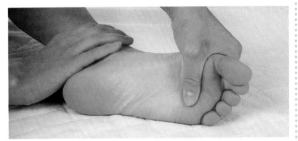

6 Squeeze the foot, loosening up the muscles and gently stretching the arch.

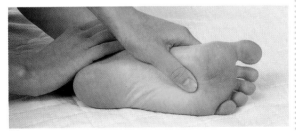

7 Use firm pressure with your thumb to stretch the foot. Repeat on the other foot.

INSTANT REVITALIZER

Do you find that you always run out of steam by 11 o'clock? Or by 4 o'clock?
Have you got to be bright and alert for a meeting, a long drive, picking up the kids or going
to a party? At any time of the day your energy can flag. Give yourself an instant "waker-upper"
with this simple yet effective routine.

1 Do a kneading action on the arms, working rapidly from the wrist to the shoulder and back again with a firm squeezing movement.

2 Knead more quickly than normal in massage, to invigorate each arm and shoulder in turn.

3 Then rub swiftly up the outside of each arm to stimulate the circulation.

4 Repeat in an upward direction each time to encourage blood flow back to the heart.

5 With the fingers and thumb of one hand, firmly squeeze the neck muscles using a circular motion.

6 With the outside edge of the hands, lightly hack on the front of each thigh, using a rapid motion.

7 Do not try to karate-chop the thighs – the hands should spring up from the muscles.

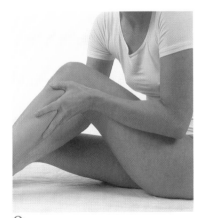

8 Next rub the calves vigorously to loosen them and get the blood moving. If possible, do this with the legs bent.

9 Always work from the ankles to the knee, using alternate hands.

10 Finally, stand up and shake your whole body, to let go of any stiffness and tension.

HEAD REVITALIZER

Almost everyone suffers from headaches at some time or another. They can have a multitude of causes, such as spending too much time in front of a computer screen, anxiety, insomnia, fatigue or sinus congestion. However, the most common cause is from tension after periods of stress. Use this simple self-massage sequence to help ease headaches, whatever their cause. You can also use it any time during the day to increase your vitality and help you to focus your mind.

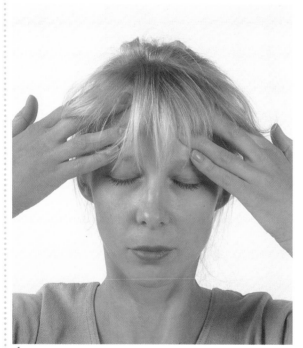

1 Use small, circling movements with the fingers, working steadily from the forehead down around the temples and over the cheeks.

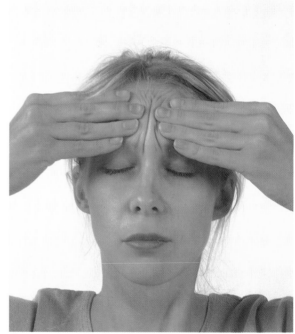

2 Use firm pressure and work slowly to ease tensions out of all the facial muscles.

3 Use your fingers to gently press around the eye socket, by your nose.

4 Smooth firmly around the arc of your eye socket beneath your brow bone.

◀ **5** Work across the cheeks and along each side of the nose, then move out to the jawline where a lot of tension is held. Try not to pull downward on the skin – let the circling movements help to smooth the stresses away and gently lift the face as you work.

CHEST AND ABDOMEN RELEASER

The front of your body is an area where emotional tension is often stored; bottling up your feelings can create tight muscles across your chest or in your abdomen. Massage treatments on these areas often trigger the release of deep-seated emotions, and need a skilled, sensitive approach. Self-massage is, however, very helpful, both in easing tense muscles and also in helping to recognize where stored tensions lie. Being aware of the effects of stress is the first step toward letting go of it. Chest muscles can ache, of course, simply through unaccustomed exercise, and this simple sequence will help.

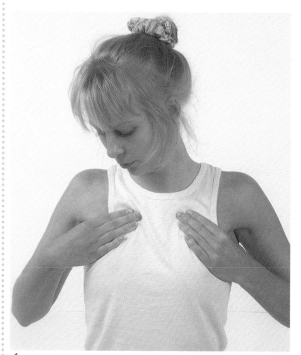

1 Using the thumb and fingers, take a good grip of the pectoral muscles, leading from the chest toward the shoulder, and knead them firmly.

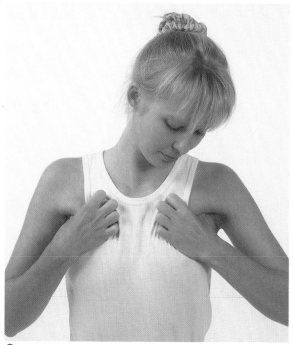

2 Be careful if you have any tenderness in the lymph glands under the armpits; women should also go gently if they have tender, swollen breasts, for example when premenstrual.

▼ **3** Using a couple of fingers, feel in between the ribs for the intercostal muscles, and work firmly along between each rib moving the fingers in tiny circles, repeating on each side.

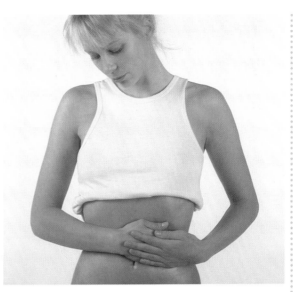

▶ **4** *Top right:* Place your hands on your abdomen, and work around slowly in a clockwise direction. If comfortable, repeat a couple of times with increasing pressure; ease off if this becomes painful.

▶ **5** By moving in this direction you encourage digestive and bowel action.

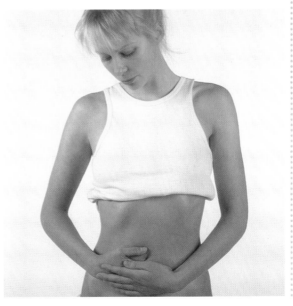

MASSAGE WITH A PARTNER

PROBABLY THE BEST WAY to improve and deepen a relationship is to increase caring physical contact, and massage is an ideal approach. The ability to ease tensions and deeply relax your partner is a very satisfying form of giving. Helping someone to release tension and feel better does not have to be limited to your life partner of course; there are other members of the family, friends or colleagues who can all be helped in this way, and a better rapport will be developed with them too.

Being massaged by someone else does mean that you can let go of your muscles more completely. It does require an amount of trust, and if you are massaging a person you do not know too well, do be sensitive to this. Massage practitioners are well aware that they are being given permission to make a deep contact with their clients, which is quite a privilege.

Take a few moments to make sure that you have created the right environment for a beneficial and relaxing massage. Check that the person is warm and comfortable, and that you have easy access to the part needing massage. Do not press harder than is comfortable for your partner and take care never to inflict pain.

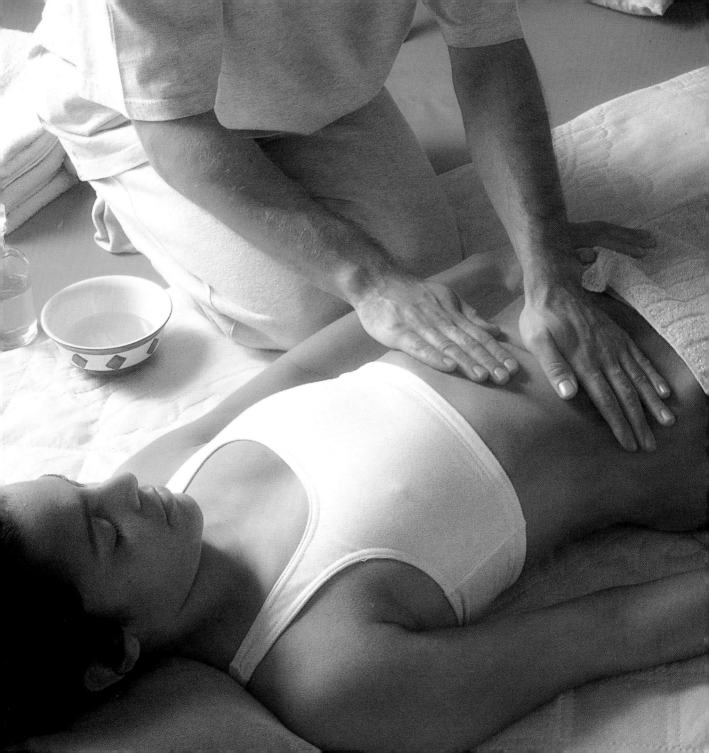

HEADACHE AND TENSION RELIEVER

One of the most common symptoms people experience when they get stressed is a tension headache; for some, this can become almost a daily pattern and may lead to migraine attacks. Any treatment should be given at the earliest stage, and massage is no exception. Just a few minutes of soothing strokes can prevent major muscle spasm and head pain.

1 Ideally, have the person lying down with his or her head in your lap, or on a cushion, while you kneel or sit just behind.

2 Using your fingertips, make alternating circles on the muscles either side of the neck.

◀ **3** Continue circling, this time with both hands working at the same time, around the sides of the head and behind the ears.

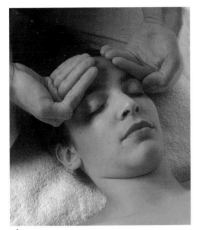

4 Smooth tension away from the temples with the backs or sides of your hands in a gentle stroking motion.

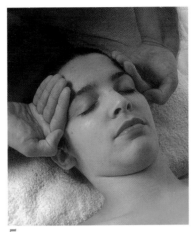

5 Gently draw the hands outwards across the forehead to soothe away worry lines.

6 Pinch and squeeze along the line of the eyebrows, reducing pressure as you work outward.

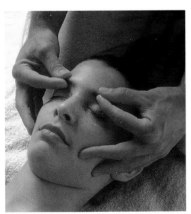

7 These muscles may be quite tender, so try not to apply too much pressure.

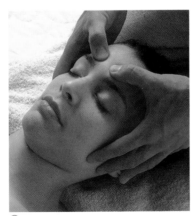

8 With your thumbs, use steady but firm pressure on the forehead, working outward from between the eyebrows.

9 Work across the brow to the hair line. This also covers many acupressure points and will release blocked energy.

SLEEP-ENHANCING FACIAL SOOTHER

If your partner has frequent problems with sleeping, or simply carries a lot of tension around in the facial muscles, this facial soother might be the answer. So why not treat your partner to this ten-minute program at bedtime? Apart from being great for relaxation, working on these muscles will smooth out worry lines and invigorate the face, making your partner look years younger – don't forget to request a facial massage for yourself in return!

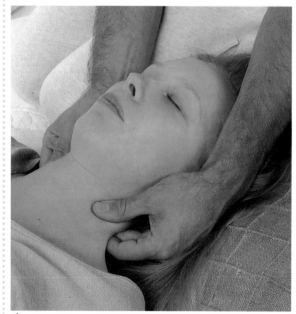

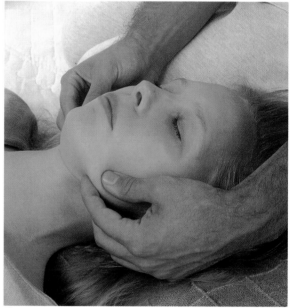

1 Kneeling behind the head, place both your hands under your partner's neck. Pull on the neck muscles gently, creating a little traction to stretch out the neck and head.

2 With your fingertips, make small circling movements along the jawline and over the cheeks. Use firm pressure, but as with all massage, avoid causing any discomfort. Try to work symmetrically, both hands moving at the same time.

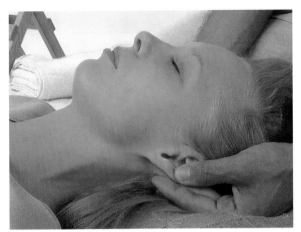

3 Pull gently with the fingertips and stretch the ears, working around from the earlobes to the top of the ears and back again.

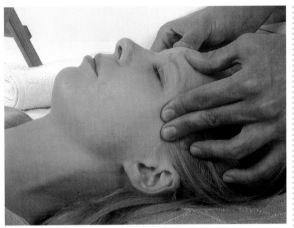

4 Apply circling movements with your fingers or thumbs on the temples and forehead, easing the pressure as you work up the temples.

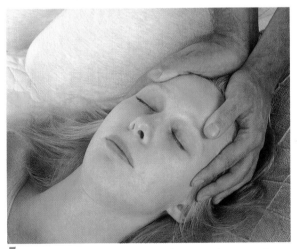

5 With the palms of your hands, smooth across the forehead, easing out tension and worry lines.

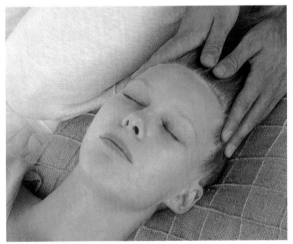

6 Continue this movement, but now working your hands toward you, and extend it by stroking up into the hair to complete the sequence.

NECK AND SHOULDER RELIEVER

Most people feel tension in their neck or shoulders at times; when you describe others – or yourself – as being uptight, it is indeed these very areas that are holding all their stresses. People who have a strong sense of responsibility are often very tense in this area, as they metaphorically "carry the world on their shoulders." Often tension in the shoulders is reflected in tight muscles lower down the back, and for a deeper effect, use the following back massage as well as the techniques described here. The muscle that takes the main brunt of tension in the shoulder is the trapezius; this is the muscle that stands out on either side when you shrug your shoulders, and it connects right up into the neck and down to the middle of the back. Lifting weights, gardening, bending over a desk and driving are typical activities that tighten the trapezius; one of the best ways to loosen it is by kneading.

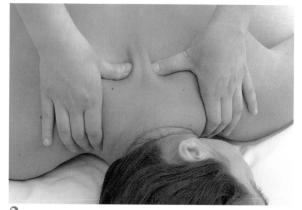

1 This technique takes a little time to master but is well worth the effort. Place both hands on the opposite shoulder, and with alternate hands squeeze your fingers and thumb together. Do not pinch, but roll the fingers over the thumb. Repeat by moving to the other side, again working on the shoulder away from your body. Ideally, get your partner to turn his or her head towards you each time, so that your fingers do not knock into the chin while kneading.

2 Having worked on each shoulder in turn, now work on both together. Place your thumbs on either side of the spine on the upper back, with the rest of each hand over each shoulder. Squeeze your fingers and thumbs together, rolling the flesh between them.

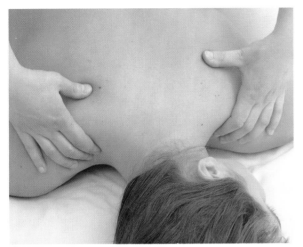

3 Let your thumbs move out smoothly across the shoulder muscles.

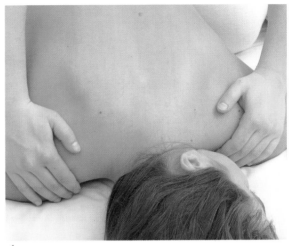

4 Release the pressure of the thumbs and stretch the blades outward with the hands.

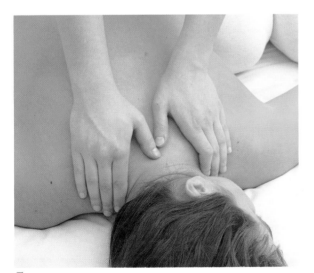

5 Return both hands to the center and get the thumbs in position to repeat.

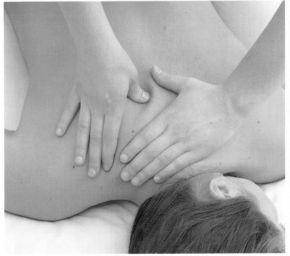

6 If the neck is very stiff, repeat the kneading, applying firmer pressure with the thumbs.

TENSION AND BACKACHE RELIEVER

The back is where most of our physical aches and pains are generally located; more days are taken off work each year because of back problems than all other parts of the body put together. It is a good area to massage, with broad, relaxing movements that cannot be carried out easily elsewhere. People can unwind, lying face down, and you may find your partner is asleep by the time you finish!

All the basic strokes are applicable to working on the back, and students in a massage class often learn many of the movements here first. Remember, if you need to apply more pressure with any movement, simply lean your whole body into the action. Try not to tense your fingers or hands as this will make the action less comfortable rather than deeper.

Apply oil smoothly to the back, remembering to put it onto your own hands before spreading it on your partner's skin, in order to warm the oil. Use enough to allow your hands to move easily over the skin without dragging, but avoid making your partner look like a professional wrestler.

1 The best initial movement is effleurage. Sit or kneel at the head end and place your hands on the back, with the thumbs close to, but not on, the spine.

2 Steadily lean forward and glide your hands down the back, keeping a steady pressure all the way.

3 Maintaining the same pressure and slow pace, take your hands out to the side and bring them back up to the shoulders.

46

4 Kneeling at the side, place your hands on the other side of the back and move them steadily in a circular motion, using overlapping circles to work up and down the back. Move to the other side and repeat the circling technique.

5 Place both hands on the opposite side of the back and use a squeezing motion, with alternate hands, to create a kneading effect.

6 The fingers and thumbs of each hand work toward each other in a kind of pinching movement, the fingers rolling over the top of the thumbs. Repeat on the other side.

7 With one hand on the side of the back nearest you, and the other hand on the opposite side, push the hands toward and then past each other to reverse their position. This makes a wringing effect as they squeeze the muscles against the spine. Move up and down the back slowly and firmly.

8 Place your hands in the center of the back and then push them away from each other, leaning forward to maintain an even pressure during this stretch.

9 Reverse the movements to create a wringing effect as the hands pass each other before stretching out the back as they push apart.

LOWER BACK RELAXER

A classic area for storing and feeling tension is in the lumbar part of the back, where it curves backwards towards the pelvis. Incorrect posture, long periods of sitting or standing, and lifting things awkwardly are just some of the many causes that can all aggravate lower back discomfort. If your partner suffers from twinges in this area, a regular massage will stretch and relax the back and help to prevent more serious pains or injury.

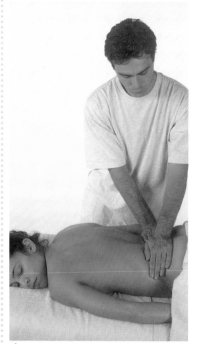

1 Standing or kneeling to the side, place your hands on the opposite side of the person's back and pull them toward you firmly and alternately.

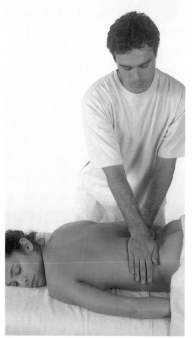

2 Overlap the hands to create an effect like bandaging – but much more soothing.

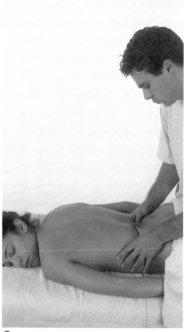

3 Using your thumbs, make circling movements over the lower back. Use a steady, even pressure, leaning with your body, but do not press on the spine.

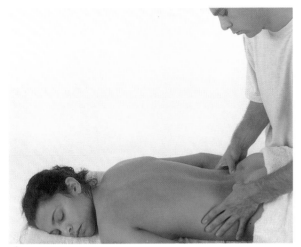

4 Stretch the lower back muscles by gliding the thumbs firmly up either side several times.

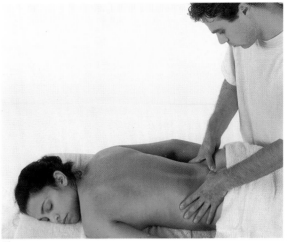

5 Press in steadily with both thumbs on either side of the spine, working slowly up it.

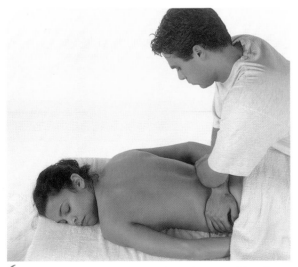

6 Stretch across the lower back with crossed hands moving away from each other, to ease taut muscles.

7 Push the hands apart and stretch the whole back.

CAUTION: Do not put any pressure on the spine itself, and ease off if it feels uncomfortable.

LEG ENERGIZER

Exercise, or lack of it, and long hours of standing or sitting, can all lead to stiff, aching leg muscles. If massaging the whole body, carry on from the back by working on the backs of the legs before getting your partner to turn over and settle comfortably again for the front.

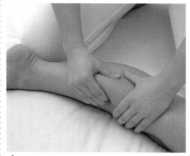

1 Knead the calves; do not apply too much pressure.

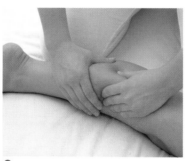

2 If possible, work up and down on the inside of the calf and then on the outside, as the muscle "splits" into two distinct halves.

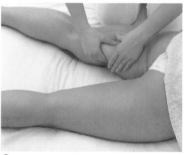

3 Knead the back of the thighs, working more to the outside to avoid the sensitive inner thigh.

4 Firm pressure with the heel of the hand up the thigh will release tight muscles.

◀ **5** Stroke smoothly and steadily up the whole back of the leg, moving the blood flow back toward the heart and draining waste matter from the muscles.

CAUTION:
Never apply any pressure directly behind the knee and never put pressure on, or squeeze, varicose veins.

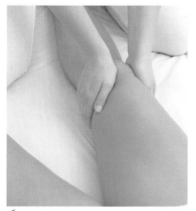

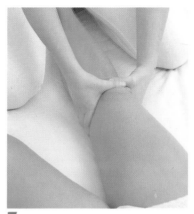

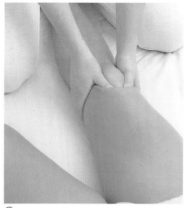

6 The front of the lower legs is mostly bone so avoid this area and move directly to the knees.

7 Make circling movements around the knees, with the thumbs. Do not put pressure directly on the kneecaps.

8 Bring the thumbs to the top of the knees and continue to circle around the edges of the kneecaps.

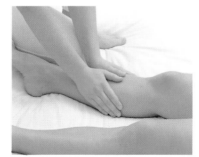

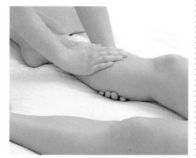

9 Kneading of the front of the thighs will help to release tight muscles and improve blood flow. Use each hand alternately, squeezing your fingers and thumb together without pinching; work more to the outside again, to avoid the sensitive inner thigh.

10 Stroke all the way up the front of the legs using both hands, always in an upward motion back toward the heart to encourage blood and lymph drainage.

11 Lighter pressure, using the flat of the palm, may be more comfortable if the veins are at all prominent. Do *not* press on varicose veins or any area of inflammation.

INSTANT FOOT REVITALIZER

With really very little complaint, your feet carry you around all day long. When you compare the size of your feet with the rest of you, it is not surprising they sometimes feel tight or sore. Relieve tired, aching feet with a ten-minute massage, and let them feel like dancing again!

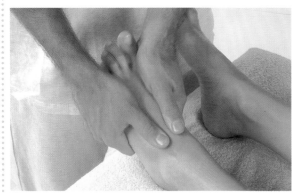

1 Hold the foot in your hands, with thumbs on top and fingers underneath.

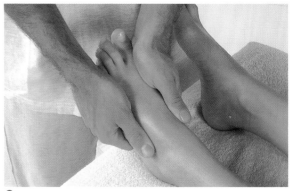

2 Gently stretch across the top of the foot; try to keep your fingers still while moving your thumbs.

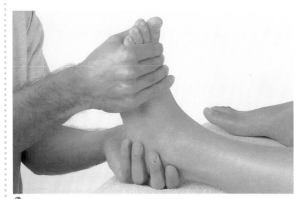

3 Flex the foot, pushing against the resistance to loosen the whole foot and ankle a little.

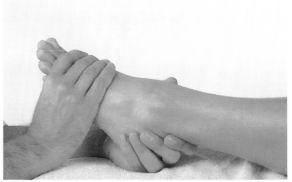

4 Then gently extend the foot, stretching it as far as is comfortable.

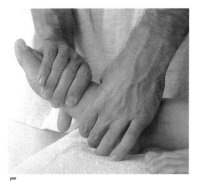

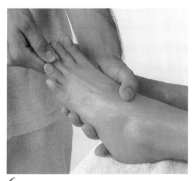

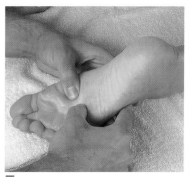

5 Twist the foot gently, using a wringing motion in both directions to stretch the muscles in every way.

6 Hold one of the toes and give a squeeze and pulling action. Repeat for all the toes.

7 Circle over the sole firmly with your fingers, or thumbs if that is easier; make sure you do not tickle your partner.

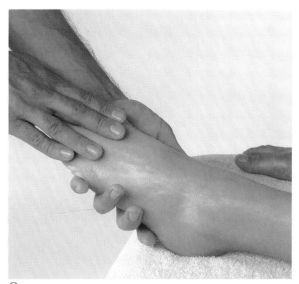

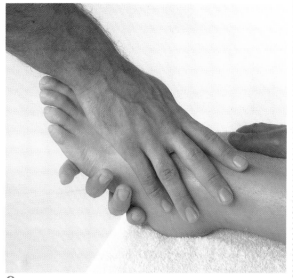

8 Support the foot with one hand and stroke the upper side with the other hand.

9 Smoothly stroke all the way from the toes to the ankle. Repeat all the actions on the other foot.

ARM AND HAND TONIC

More than any other part of your body, you use your hands and arms for all kinds of physical tasks – at work, for household chores or in leisure activities. As a result, they are often stiff and tense; a few simple massage techniques can help to shed the tensions and burdens of the day.

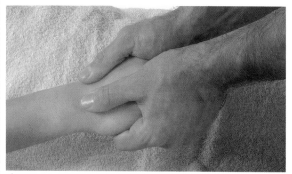

1 Kneel by your partner, who is lying face up. Hold your partner's hand, palm down, in both of your hands and with your thumbs apply a steady stretching motion across the back of the hand.

2 Repeat a few times, with a firm but comfortable pressure. Turn the hand over and use your thumbs to smooth and stretch the palm in a similar action.

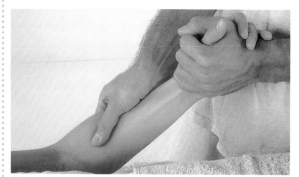

3 Squeeze the forearm, using your hand and thumb to work from the wrist toward the elbow.

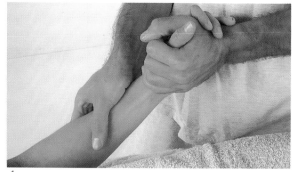

4 Repeat the motion, moving all around the arm to squeeze all the muscles.

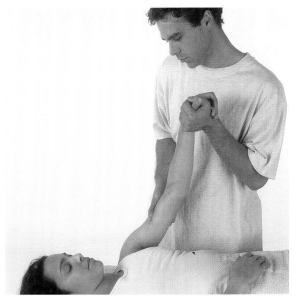

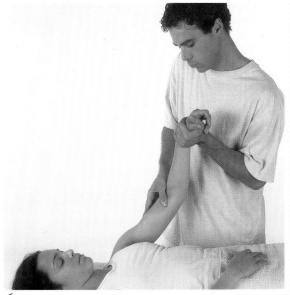

5 Lift the arm up, and then use a similar squeezing movement to work down the upper arm, from the elbow to the shoulder.

6 Repeat, working all around the arm. Switch hands if necessary for a more comfortable action. Repeat all these movements on the other arm.

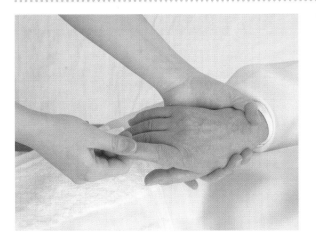

◀ Older people often find that their fingers are not as dextrous as they once were. As long as the joints are not inflamed or in a degenerated condition, a regular hand massage with gentle movements and finger stretches will aid continued flexibility.

TENSE ABDOMEN RELIEVER

Tension in the abdomen may reflect some physical discomfort, such as indigestion, constipation or menstrual cramps. Often, though, people hold their inner fears and anxieties in this area. If you bottle up your feelings, then you can become literally unable to digest stress, and abdominal spasms may occur. Try these movements, working slowly and just as deeply as feels comfortable to your partner.

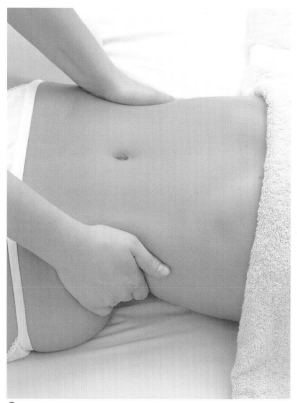

1 Kneeling by the side, slide your hands under the back to meet at the spine. Lift the body to arch the back before pulling your hands out toward the hips.

2 Firmly draw your hands over the waist and then gently glide them back to their original position to repeat the stroke.

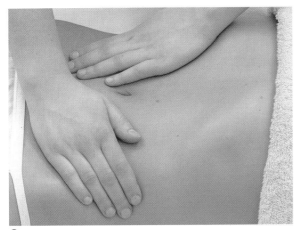

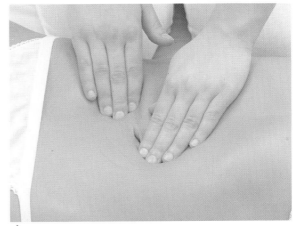

3 Placing your hands on the abdomen, move them around steadily in a clockwise direction (this follows the way in which the colon functions).

4 Repeat the action, working a little deeper by using your fingers if there is no discomfort.

5 Place your hands on the abdomen, over the navel, and simply try to make your hands and arms as relaxed as possible. Focus calming thoughts down through your own body into your partner. You may be surprised at how effective this simple technique can be in helping to relax tense muscles.

OFFICE MASSAGE: DE-STRESS YOUR COLLEAGUES

Massage is a highly versatile skill and can be applied in many situations. How often have you heard one of your work colleagues complain of tense, aching shoulders or back? Well, now you can do something about it – a five-minute massage can be wonderfully effective at refreshing and reenergizing people. No special equipment is needed, and you can work on people when they are fully clothed and still seated at their desks.

1 Standing behind your seated colleague, place your hands on both shoulders, thumbs towards you and fingers in the front.

2 Knead both shoulders at the same time, with a firm squeezing movement; adjust your pressure to the amount of clothing and to the degree of discomfort felt.

3 Using your fingers, knead in small circles up and down the back of the neck. Try to support the head with your other hand while you are working on the neck.

4 Place your forearms over the shoulders and press down with your body weight to squeeze and stretch the trapezius muscles.

5 Move the forearms outward to the shoulders, keeping a firm pressure all the time.

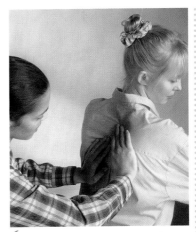

6 Using your fingers, make firm circling motions down the back, to one side of the spine.

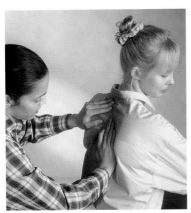

7 Allow the fingers to sink into the muscles around the shoulder blade. Repeat on the other side.

8 Place your hands on your partner's shoulder joints and press back toward yourself to stretch the upper chest.

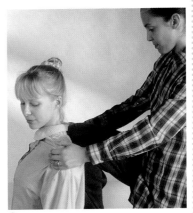

9 With care and balance, you can do this stretch with your leg pressing into your colleague's back.

LIBIDO ENHANCER: SENSUAL MASSAGE

As well as releasing stresses and tensions from the muscles, massage is a wonderful way to enhance a relationship, by increasing caring, sharing touch. If your relationship seems to have got into a rut, and sexual energy is low, why not revitalize yourselves with some soothing massage strokes. It is important to take a little extra time to create the right environment, to make the whole experience a real treat – time for you both in a hurried world. Make the room extra warm, get your partner to be minimally clothed or to undress fully, and just be covered with warm towels, perhaps play some of your favorite, soothing music and have soft lighting or better still, work in candle light. Stroking movements should be the mainstay of a sensual massage. Use a little more oil than usual to help them flow more easily. At the end, your partner may, of course, just fall asleep.

1 Effleurage is a classic stroking movement. Place your hands on either side of the spine, but not on it, and glide down the back. Move out to the sides and up the back again. Repeat several times.

2 With a gentle motion, stroke down the center of the back with one hand following the other smoothly, as if you were stroking a cat.

3 As one hand lifts off at the pelvis, start again with the other hand at the neck.

4 Place both your hands on the upper back and stroke outward in a fan shape.

5 Work down the back, including the buttocks, using the fanning action.

6 Use a firm, steady circling action on the buttocks. These are large, powerful muscles that may be able to take a little more pressure if your partner desires, but avoid giving any discomfort.

7 Stroke up the back of the legs, with one hand after the other, in a smooth, flowing motion.

8 As one hand reaches the buttocks, start on the calf with the other to keep a steady rhythm.

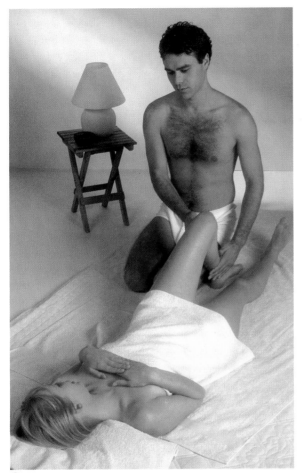

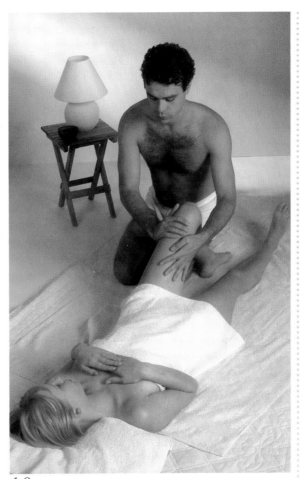

9 Turn your partner over and stroke up the front of the legs; having the legs bent helps the muscles relax.

10 Continue the movement, using both hands to stroke from the knees up the thighs.

11 Effleurage may also be used on the front of the body, kneeling from the head end. Be careful not to press in with your thumbs. All these movements should make for a truly sensual experience and help to put your partner back in touch with his or her body – and maybe yours too.

INDEX

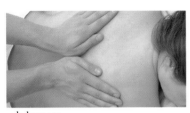

Photography Acknowledgments
The publishers would like to
credit the following photogra-
phers: Alistair Hughes (p. 6, 10,
11, 14, 17, 18, 19, 20, 21, 22, 23,
44, 45, 46, 47, 50, 51, 56, 57);
Lucy Mason (p. 15).

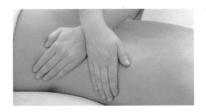